AUG **26** 2019

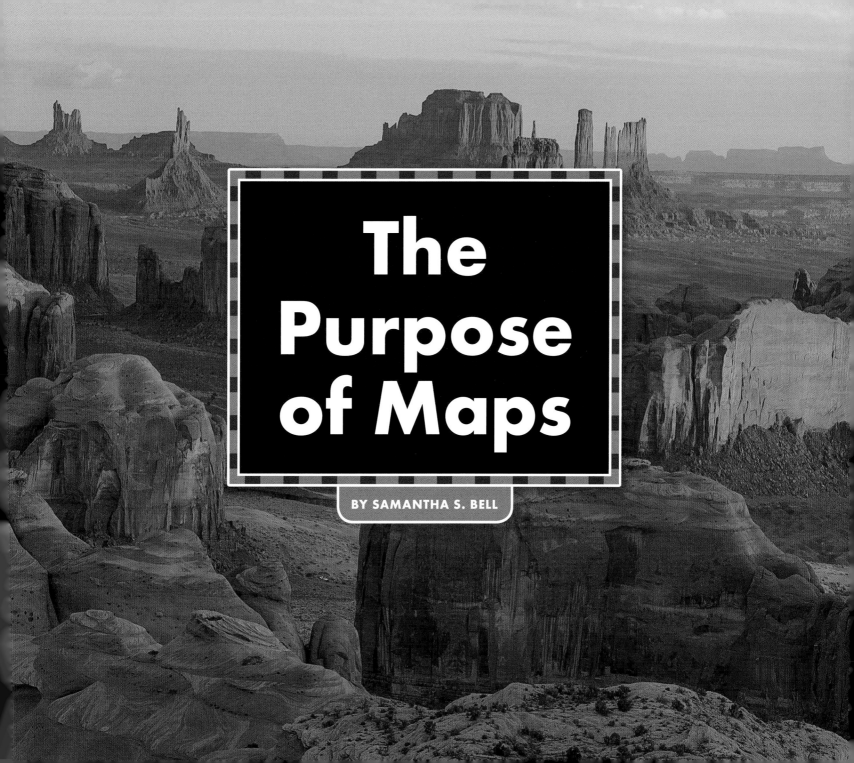

# The Purpose of Maps

BY SAMANTHA S. BELL

**The Child's World®**
childsworld.com

Published by The Child's World®
1980 Lookout Drive • Mankato, MN 56003-1705
800-599-READ • www.childsworld.com

Photographs ©: Photographs ©: Shutterstock
Images, cover (foreground); Zhukova Valentyna/
Shutterstock Images, cover (background),
1; iStockphoto, 5; Hurst Photo/Shutterstock
Images, 6; Sergey Novikov/Shutterstock
Images, 9; Nadya Eugene/Shutterstock Images,
10; Serban Bogdan/Shutterstock Images,
13; Monkey Business Images/Shutterstock
Images, 15; wavebreakmedia/Shutterstock
Images, 16; KiskaMedia/iStockphoto, 18

ISBN Hardcover: 9781503827851
ISBN Paperback: 9781622434527
LCCN: 2018944817

Printed in the United States of America
PA02397

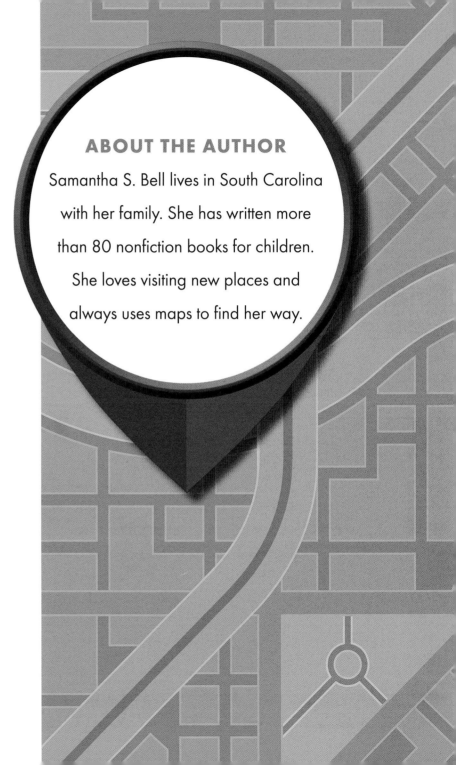

## ABOUT THE AUTHOR

Samantha S. Bell lives in South Carolina with her family. She has written more than 80 nonfiction books for children. She loves visiting new places and always uses maps to find her way.

# TABLE OF CONTENTS

# CHAPTER ONE

# We Need Maps

Your family is taking a trip! You are going somewhere you have never been before. Your parents show you where you are going on a map. They will use the map to get there. It will show them which way to go.

A map is usually drawn on a flat surface. It shows all or part of Earth. Everything on the map is drawn to **scale**.

You can use maps to find your way in places you've never visited before.

Maps can show many different places.

A map might show the whole world. You can see the **continents** and countries. You can see the oceans and large rivers.

A map might show one country. You can see the states and large cities. Some maps show only cities. You can see the roads and **landmarks**.

Mapmakers are called cartographers. They make maps for many different purposes.

Maps are easy to store and carry. Some are made of paper. Others are **digital**. They all provide information for people to use.

# CHAPTER TWO

# General Purpose Maps

General purpose maps show where things are located. They tell us what can be found in a certain area.

Some general purpose maps are called political maps. Political maps have lines called **boundaries**. Some boundaries separate countries. Some separate states.

A general purpose map can show where different things are in a city.

Some political maps also show the location of cities. When you find your hometown on a map, you are using a political map.

Some general purpose maps are called physical maps. They show **natural** features. They show what the land is like.

Physical maps show mountains and forests. They show deserts. They show lakes and rivers, too.

Some physical maps are called topographic maps. They show how high or low the land is. They show all of the hills and valleys. Some general purpose maps have all of these features. They give us information about both the places and the land.

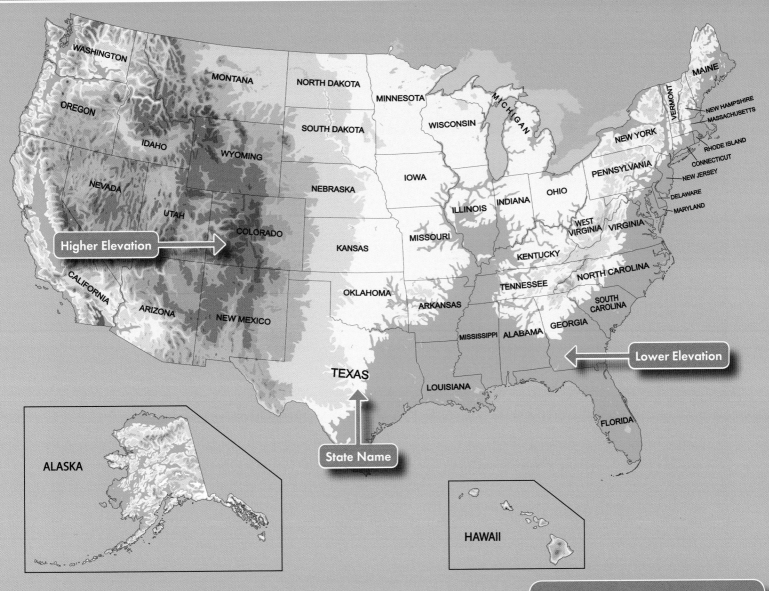

WASHINGTON
OREGON
IDAHO
MONTANA
NORTH DAKOTA
MINNESOTA
WISCONSIN
MICHIGAN
MAINE
VERMONT
NEW HAMPSHIRE
MASSACHUSETTS
NEW YORK
RHODE ISLAND
CONNECTICUT
NEW JERSEY
PENNSYLVANIA
DELAWARE
MARYLAND
SOUTH DAKOTA
WYOMING
NEVADA
UTAH
COLORADO
IOWA
NEBRASKA
OHIO
INDIANA
ILLINOIS
MISSOURI
KANSAS
WEST VIRGINIA
VIRGINIA
KENTUCKY
NORTH CAROLINA
TENNESSEE
SOUTH CAROLINA
OKLAHOMA
ARKANSAS
CALIFORNIA
ARIZONA
NEW MEXICO
MISSISSIPPI
ALABAMA
GEORGIA
TEXAS
LOUISIANA
FLORIDA

**Higher Elevation** →

← **Lower Elevation**

↑ **State Name**

ALASKA

HAWAII

This map is a physical map of the United States. It shows the natural features of the United States.

# CHAPTER THREE

# Thematic and Special Purpose Maps

Thematic and special purpose maps focus on one subject or **theme**. There are many kinds of thematic and special purpose maps.

Population maps show how many people live in an area. Other maps show what kinds of food people grow or the things they make.

Seeing a population map can help us understand where people live.

Climate maps help us know when to plant gardens.

Some maps provide information about wildlife. They may show what kinds of plants live in an area. They may show where animals travel.

**Climate** maps show the weather conditions in a certain place. They may show how much **precipitation** has fallen. They may show the temperature. They could also show what kind of weather might be coming.

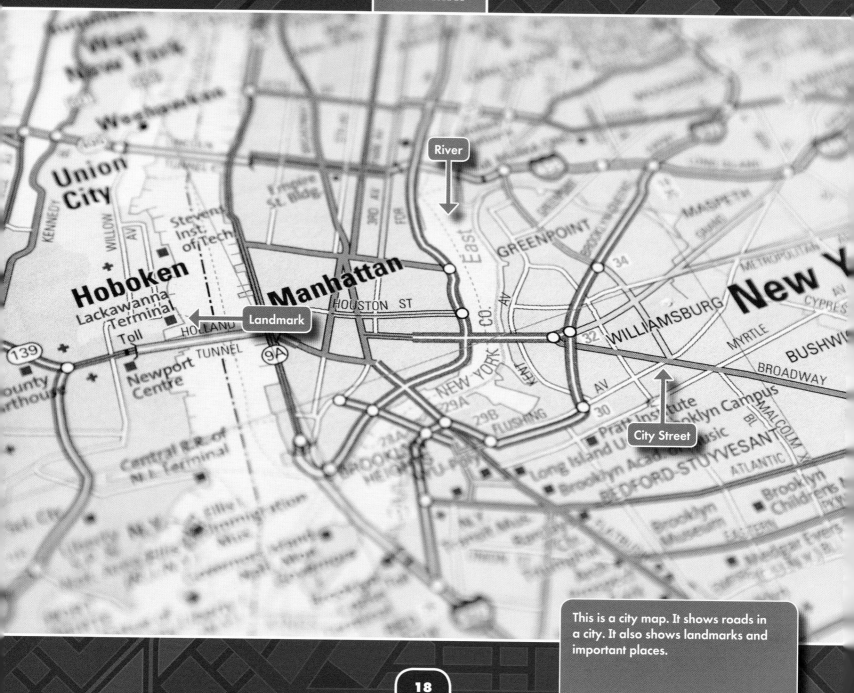

River

Landmark

City Street

This is a city map. It shows roads in a city. It also shows landmarks and important places.

Road maps show all of the roads in a certain area. They may also show businesses and homes. They help people find their way from one place to another.

We use maps for many different reasons. They tell us about places and people. They help us learn more about our world.

# Do You Know?

**Q:** What are mapmakers called?

**A:** Cartographers

**Q:** What kind of map shows natural features like mountains and deserts?

**A:** Physical maps

**Q:** What is a boundary?

**A:** A line that separates counties on a map.

**Q:** What do climate maps tell us about?

**A:** Climate maps tell us about the weather in a specific place.

**Q:** When would you use a road map?

**Q:** Can you think of a time you would use a specific map?

# Glossary

**boundaries** (BOWN-duh-reez) Boundaries are dividing lines that show the end or limit of something. Some maps show the boundaries between states.

**climate** (KLYE-mit) Climate refers to the weather conditions of a certain region. The climate in Florida is hot in the summer.

**continents** (KON-tuh-nuhntz) Contients are the large divisions of land on a map of Earth, including North America, South America, Europe, Asia, Australia, Antarctica, and Africa. World maps show all the continents.

**digital** (DIJ-uh-tuhl) Digital refers to something that uses electronic or computer technology. Some people use digital maps on their cell phones.

**landmarks** (LAND-markz) Landmarks are important buildings or monuments. The Lincoln Memorial and the White House are landmarks in Washington, DC.

**natural** (NACH-ur-uhl) Natural refers to something that exists in or is produced by nature. The Grand Canyon is a natural feature seen on some maps.

**precipitation** (pri-sip-i-TAY-shuhn) Precipitation is water that falls to the earth as hail, mist, rain, snow, or sleet. Weather reports tell how much precipitation falls in a certain area.

**scale** (SKAYL) Scale refers to the ratio of a distance on a map to the corresponding distance on the ground. Maps that are accurate are drawn to scale.

**theme** (THEEM) A theme is a specific focus or subject matter of a map. A map theme can be weather, population, languages, or jobs.

# To Learn More

### BOOKS

Hewitt, Sally. *Maps*. Mankato, MN: Amicus, 2011.

Mizielinska, Aleksandra, and Daniel Mizielinski. *Maps*.
Somerville, MA: Candlewick Press, 2013.

Olien, Rebecca. *Looking at Maps and Globes*.
New York, NY: Children's Press, 2013.

### WEB SITES

Visit our Web site for links about the purpose of maps:
**childsworld.com/links**

*Note to Parents, Teachers, and Librarians: We routinely verify our Web links to make sure
they are safe and active sites. So encourage your readers to check them out!*

# Index